ABOUT VERVE POETRY FESTIVAL

Verve isn't your typical literary festival. Still only four years old, it has already made a huge mark on the national poetry scene, noted for its:
    Roof-shaking spoken word sets
    Readings and workshops by award-winning poets
    Boundary-pushing poetry/theatre performances
    Lively children's events
    and much, much more!
Most importantly, Verve is a festival for everyone to enjoy poetry together - where performance poets and page poets mingle and appreciate each others' art, where experimental poets swap numbers with childrens poets. Verve is for beginners and seasoned poetry afficiandos and everything in between. What ever kind of poet or poetry fan you are, no-one gets left out at Verve!

http://vervepoetryfestival.com
enquiries@vervepoetryfestival.com

We've Done Nothing Wrong. We've Nothing To Hide.

The Verve Anthology of Diversity Poems

VERVE
POETRY PRESS
BIRMINGHAM

PUBLISHED BY VERVE POETRY PRESS
https://vervepoetrypress.com
mail@vervepoetrypress.com

All rights reserved
© 2020 all individual authors

The right of all individuals to be identified as author if this work has been asserted in accordance with section 77 of the Copyright, Designs and Patents Act 1988.

No part of this work may be reproduced, stored or transmitted in any form or by any means, graphic, electronic, recorded or mechanical, without the prior written permission of the publisher.

FIRST PUBLISHED FEB 2020

Printed and bound in the UK
by Imprint Digital, Exeter

ISBN: 978-1-912565-34-4

The title *We've Dont Nothing Wrong, We've Nothing to Hide* has been borrowed from Claire Collison's poem *Beach of the Asymmetrics* which is included in these pages.

To difference - to communication - to understanding.

CONTENTS

Foreword By The Verve Team
Introduction by Andrew McMillan

Beach of the Asymmetrics - Claire Collison	15
Pest Control - C.I. - Kat Payne Ware	16
The Dogs - Eleanor Penny	17
The Girl in the Pink Raincoat - Jhilmil Breckenridge	18
Ode to a Hanging Basket - Michael Saunderson	20
We're all in someone else's story - Christpher M James	22
Gaylord - Jack Parlett	23
Home Movie - Hilary Watson	25
The Announcement - Stephanie Papa	26
Acute Admissions Ward - Natalie Crick	28
How to Wheel - Karl Knights	29
Don't Say Firstborn - Prerana Kumar	30
Calamity Jane - Thomas Stewart	32
the first rule of ventriloquism club - Paul Howarth	33
Locker Room Porn - Samuel Green	34

exquisite corpse - Jack Cooper	36
Common - Natalie Whittaker	37
A poem for Alina that is not called 'Rain' - Tim Kiely	38
Valencia - Estelle Birdy	40
The Hepworth - Maria Leonard	42
Big and Clever - Miles Fagge	44
life is good beneath the leaves - Shaun Hill	45
Butch - Roma Havers	46
Plantain - Isabelle Baafi	48
the bull symbol in 'A' - Jade Cuttle	50
Journal Fragments '82 - Dale Booton	54
The Gift Shop Elegies #9: Elegy with Exhibition Booklet for 'Coming Out: Sexuality, Gender & Identity' (Walker Art Gallery, Liverpool; Birmingham Museum and Art Gallery) - Zosia Kuczyńska	57
Dust - Jemima Hughes	62

Notes & Acknowledgements

FOREWORD

The quality of the entries to our annual Verve Festival competitions never fails to surprise and delight us. This year, with the theme of Diversity (what better for a festival with diversity at its heart?) we are again as thrilled as can be with the winning and commended poems chosen by Andrew McMillan and included here. They are as varied in form and content as you might expect, but they do have something in common - a certain feeling that diverse approaches to love and life aren't to be celebrated. Not yet. Instead these poems sound more like dispatches from lives that are regularly misunderstood and misrepresented. But the attempt at communication is the important thing here. The more we hear, the more we understand, the more we share, the more we will accept and celebrate. There is work to be done. Let this anthology be part of that work, and move things forward.

Alongside and among these chosen poems are three poems that were commissioned for this anthology and the companion event from poets with links to the festival. Again you couldn't hope for three more varied approaches to the same brief both in form, content and length. Jhilmil Breckenridge, Shaun Hill and Jemima Hughes are at different stages of their poetry journey and all have wonderful poetry futures ahead of them.

We know you will enjoy these poems. Share them about too. Let's get these messages heard and savoured. Let's keep the conversation going.

The Verve Team
Stuart, Lizzie, Kibriya, Nellie

INTRODUCTION

I've decided, and not just because I'm feeling particularly sorry for myself this morning, that judging a poetry competition can feel a lot like having flu. You're confronted with so many poems the mind can feel slightly fogged, you can feel stuffed up with language, bunged up with images and similes, and then, every so often, there's a poem or a phrase or a line that feels like a dollop of vicks vapour rub- suddenly there is clarity, things lift, you can see clearly, the poem has cleared everything, and shown you a way through.

There was a tissue-box full of different themes and ideas in the submissions which were made to this competition. I'm aware of my reputation, of the sort of poetry I'm known for writing, and so there were a lot of poems which spoke directly to those themes. Equally though, there were poems which I loved because they were so unlike anything I might ever write (a poem in praise of hanging baskets!) or poems I could never write (from the experience of a disabled body living in the world). As a poet, I love the things I can't do, just as much as what I can. It's impossible to judge poems against each other, all you can do, as I know I've said before (I'm groggy, I'm phlegmy , forgive me for repeating myself), is to judge them against what they were trying to do for themselves, could they have done it better.

Each poem in a process like this gets put through the wringer, we try and see how much it withstand the constant re-reading, how much can each line stand up to interrogation and study. Some poems tear easily, like a cheap tissue, some poems feel strong, but the more you read, what at first seemed like strength comes to seem like flashy showmanship. The best poems are the ones that keep their strength, and indeed keep growing and expanding the more you re-read them.

All of these winning poems and highly commended poems stayed with me, like an undissolvable throat-lozenge, long after re-reading. I think there's something too, about a theme of diversity, which meant many of these poems were dispatches from voices we should be hearing much more of in poetry.

About the winners

1st Prize- The Dogs
In this arresting prose poem, there is a sense of myth or folk-tale about the language, and yet something utterly contemporary and fresh as well. That tension, or that push and pull between the two types of language in the poem mean that there's a tension in the poem that makes it feel as though it vibrates on the page. I couldn't tell you everything that's going on in this poem, but I'm not sure that matters, it's a poem I need to keep spending time with, need to keep re-reading; it opens itself up and expands more with each reading.

2nd Prize- Gaylord
There's a subtly to the poem which isn't necessarily expected if one just looked at the title. Something about the short, staccato lines, but the constant enjambment as well, gives the poem a jagged feel but also a forward propulsion. A lot of young queer boys (and others) from a certain generation will recognise themselves in this poem I think, and yet, in its pointed epigraph, we also see how this poem is speaking out to wider socio-political issues as well. Poems like this are hard to get right (I know, I try and fail to write a lot of them myself) how much do you withhold, how much do you explain or show; it feels as though this poem gets the perfect balance.

3rd Prize- How to Wheel
One of the joys of judging this prize was that, more than others I've judged, there was a lot of work which felt it was coming from the disabled experience. Perhaps it was the theme, perhaps just coincidence, but I was delighted to read all of them and this poem in particular. It's a deceptively simple piece, which describes a moment in time, and yet manages to open out to say something about ability and perception as well. The use of verbs in this poem, swing for example, is perfectly on point, and is one of the real triumphs of a poem which reveals its depths each time we revisit.

Andrew McMillan
The Verve 2020 Competition Judge.

We've Done Nothing Wrong.
We've Nothing To Hide.

Beach of the Asymmetrics
Claire Collison

You're a young man with one leg; the rest is conture. Because this is Portsmouth, I surmise soldier. Because of your age, Iraq. You are swinging to the shore. You steady yourself; throwing the crutches onto the sand; drop, and drag yourself into the sea. From here on, you are no different. Later, drying off, you chat to other bathers, whose demeanour towards you I read as respectful.

Because I'm a pacifist, because I don't see cancer as a battle, I'm surprised to be learning from a soldier: it's not our fault. We did nothing wrong. We've nothing to hide.

Pest Control
Kat Payne Ware

My last week in Berlin, the pigeons died.
They dropped from trees like autumn come too soon,
littered pavements (which Germans despise),
twitching bodies taking up the room.
Pedestrians formed tiptoed pantomime
(eyes wide, finger on lips, *he's behind you*) –
still, feathers clung like children to our thighs
and drifted through the dark parts of the dorm.

Back page of the in-flight magazine:
kids, puffed like pool floats in their winter clothes,
reach Calais, silent conga line, unseen,
then topple down like tenpins in the road.
They'd made it in a freezer container.

In my suitcase wheel: a grey feather.

The Dogs
Eleanor Penny

after Helen Mort

Before you were born your mother too was visited by dogs. They asked her how she kept the hair from her eyes when she committed small atrocities. What blood type was her blood type. How her neck smelled in the rain. They told her it's not wrong to want a child who fights for its food. Sinks its teeth into the ankle of the world. Sleeps in the sun, vendetta-less, untroubled by strange men. Spit from its jaws pooling on the stone for anyone to see. It's alright to want a child who will recognise its name. Who will come home when you call it. She ate coal in the back garden, squatting by the bucket, furnace-handed. Brittle-tongued. She couldn't spell the word belief, but every day she practised. Ate without her hands. Cut her palms on street glass. Healed quickly. Patched up each violation. She learned to want some kind of child who would answer to its name. At least you know now. Show her you can sink your teeth into something and hold on. Fill her house with howling. Dig up flower bulbs and chicken bones and bring them to her door. It was morning when at last she ran with the dogs. She ran to the gutters and gave birth there in the gasping light, bloodwaters sluicing off into the drain. Still across the city she is calling. At least now you know.

The Girl In The Pink Raincoat
Jhilmil Breckenridge

The 12.16 Crewe to London train sits on Platform 11 like a hungry beast ready to roar. I get on, paratha and sabzi in a small bundle in my red backpack. Like Indian travellers of long ago, I'm carrying my next meal with me, more for health reasons, less because of habit—you never know with Indian trains. I remember the grimy platforms of my childhood, the smell of coal, the man saying chai-chai.

Here in England, everything is sterile and clean. The Pumpkin Cafe on the corner is selling sandwiches made in a sterile and clean factory far away. A woman wearing a red beret sips her latte while a young man with tattoos on his neck laughs on his phone.

The bundle of food in my bag is calling. I worry about the Indian spices, the strong smells. But no one is sitting near me and my stomach growls. I open my round steel tiffin with two parathas, another plastic box with okra, freshly made this morning, tempered with cumin seeds and red chillies. It's still warm. The spicy aroma fills the West Midlands train; it's green seats look at me balefully. I want to finish eating before anyone gets on. We still have still eight minutes before departure.

A young mother, her blonde hair perfectly highlighted gets on with a little girl in a pink plastic raincoat. Her purple and pink boots run to the seats on my right and they settle in. The mother's jeans are ripped at the knee and her nail polish is chipped. I continue eating quickly, closing the box of okra with every bite so it would be less smelly, less fragrant, less obvious.

Just then, the little girl asks her mother, Mum, what's that smell? The mother looks at me and says Food, I think. I look at the little girl. Food, I say, slightly tentative. You want to come see?

She scampers over, her purple boots, her pink raincoat, her blue eyes trusting. She peers into the box of paratha and extends her hand in to taste. Would you like some, I ask? Shyly she nods. I break off a small piece, roll it up like I did for my kids, and hand it to her. She looks at the okra but I say, *No, too spicy. Chillies.* She hops back to her seat.

And she eats, licking her fingers, saying yum yum. I smile. Her mother laughs. I let the box of okra stay open.

This is how the world can be. Like her eyes. Open and trusting. Every day, the world presents us with opportunities to be more separate, more foreign. And every day, a little girl reminds us we are all the same.

Ode to a Hanging Basket
Michael Saunderson

What black-capped judge
sentenced you to hang
by three chains until dead?

On what ground
did the barrister
build his case -

overcrowded housing,
holding roots hostage in a confined space,
weaving baskets for entrapment,
domestic violence under the influence
of a brisk summer wind?

How could a jury be formed
so impervious
to your impassioned defence?

How your blooms were saved
from suffocating at birth
in polystyrene cribs.

How your trailing stems
form arms of friendship
to a passing world -

your contribution to multi-colourism,
your constant supply of young heads for old,
your nightly sequestration of a little more carbon,
your food bank for insects,
your beautiful refraction of sunlight.

Outwit the dead heading!
Force out from containment
with every ounce of nutrient you find.
Invigorate our world
for the full length of your season.

We're all in someone else's story
Christopher M James

Chiang Mai, Thailand

When we moved in, our German neighbour was already dying. He'd been tending his garden for ten years. Got up from his bed once to visit. Told us we were paying too much rent. And his wife was some sort of saint. And we should be sure to lock the gates when out. Told us he was the surviving, secret grandson of Hitler. His grandfather the carpenter at the *Berghof* in *Obersalzberg*. I listened, lost for words. Or references. We pocket narratives like expired membership cards. Mountain passes in heads. At his cremation, his tattooed biker friend helped to bear the coffin.

But the usual firecrackers seemed oddly inappropriate.

Months later, when cold nights threw us off the days' trail, he came back to me. I lay down and dreamed an old tale. He was the captain of my ship, staring at the pin-cushion stars. My brother and I, on the deck, were going to a faraway island. All the inhabitants had it. One single eye in the middle of their foreheads. We'd hatched a plan. Go to the island. Capture a few one-eyed specimens. Bring them back, sell them to a zoo. Make a sure fortune... They must have seen us coming. We landed on the beach. A group of one-eyed men accosted us. Captured my brother and I. Sold us to the zoo. The zoo on the island.

Gaylord
Jack Parlett
for Andrea Leadsom

Baked beans
school meals
hot dog days
playing ball
& hearing
isn't he a nice
boy, puffed up
and quiet
sensitive even
friends with girls
a 'bookish' type
seen singing
Will Young
by the goalposts
piquing suspicions
among straight
talking mums.
"One day this kid"
camp before his time
will process this hurt
in some queer poetry
workshop. Smiling
will go home to kiss
his boyfriend
in unknown places;
limp-wristed
and ham-fisted

will laugh away
your scorn
through pink
and zealous tears,
bowing in thanks
for the other voices
to which he was
exposed

Home Movie
Hilary Watson
after Danez Smith

Let's make a home movie about the time we held
hands in the street and someone screamed GAY
in our faces. Let's call it *All the Reasons I'm different
from you* and *No you can't have 'straight pride'* &
*Why you can't have lesbians at your wedding
who feel totally fine about being there*. Remember
when correctional rape was a thing, like it's not still
a thing, like the apology that pings through from you
before your friend sends a photograph of your face
with unicorn-coloured cocks entering your mouth.
Remember when she wanted to get pregnant so we sent
a photo of her body with a cartoon womb cut out? No,
nor do I. Do you sense disgust now? Let's make a home movie
about the time we held hands until we stepped outside.
We'll cast the character of Distance as Andy Serkis
leering from my foot to yours for our safety.
In my home movie we are going to be naked chickens
in a farmhouse near Poppit Sands. I'll call it *Ghost Tracks*
and no one will dare ask who's queer. The reel will end
with us running down to the surf in our flamboyant feathers,
avoiding jellyfish beached like gelatine whales.

The Announcement
Stephanie Papa

Still now infinite nights of his journey,
Sudan, Libya, Italy, Calais, Paris,
wake up and rise in his mouth.
The drivers would beat us,
he says today.
We'd pay them to get us there
And they'd beat us.
More often though, fields of words
wait inside, not making a sound.

He laughs at a red squirrel
scribbling up an oak— *écureuil*
he repeats—admires a mother
trailing a wagon of children
strapped to her bike.
Trees breathe, reflect in his eyes.

I will visit Sudan again, he says.
Why, I ask, if they're killing people,
throwing them, feet bound, into the Nile.
If there is a protest, he says,
I will take another road,
and one day you'll come with me.
We talk about the Nubian pyramids again.
The forest stops to take our picture.

I ask after his girlfriend in Khartoum,
her pink headscarf framing her face,
hands painted with henna.
There is a baby coming soon, he says.
This is why I will go.
It took him years to speak to me like this
and from this sentence everything grows,
lush vines climb out of his chest,
yes a baby, he repeats,
proud, all of his cells offering me flowers.

Acute Admissions Ward
Natalie Crick

If silence were a building
it would be a mental hospital
during the Christmas holidays,
when you are told you cannot
leave. I'm told a house is
waiting out there in silence,
with a nurse and an alarm.
We are dissociates in flowered
pyjamas who lick our Wish Food.
Our faces are mineral in colour.
This silence is blue rain, stirring
the dirt in our brains. (The silence
of long sleeps, the silence of thick
shells, the silence of white pills).
Silence is the taste of tongue, teeth
and lips mangled inside a death star
where thoughts are cut soft and grey
at the root. Tardive Dyskinesia,
nooses and matches.

How to Wheel
Karl Knights

The zoo is tough terrain; hilly.
I wheel as fast as I can
then mum shouts 'keep up!'
I stop. 'Hand me my crutches.'
I shakily get up; take off my splints
strap by strap, and put them on her.
I sit her in the chair. 'You have a go.'

At first, she spins in circles.
No, I say. Use both arms in unison.
She still veers away, zigzagging, sweating now.
People start to stare. She blushes,
keeps her head down. After an hour
she's heaving, shirt drenched. I swing over to her.

Don't Say Firstborn
Prerana Kumar

Say first advance.   into everything.
head first fall.   first said no.
say how do we forgive ourselves
for not being sons ?

Say stop. say how family
fell - like torn confetti
on the first bib- shaped birthday cake.
say scorch tongue,   swollen tight.
everyone else's apology smeared
hot cream.

Say aunty   cried when breasts first bloomed.
Say open   wide. devour gold clink bangles piled
for the wedding. firstborn daughter stomachs bursting
with dowry.

Say everything wept indigo
at mother's slit. how we died
in a heart.
Say how we forgotten battle - horse,
echoes of arrow-rust knocking in knees.
Say we were traded for fresh chariot.
Say we so wrong delivered. feet first tumble.
half-retch on puncture caul.
how   we gasped disappointment
after first cry.
Say we breech
offering.

Say cease. say no, we first line defence.
first to bite hornet's nest. we crack
back door at dawn.   creep on gash knees
to gold speckled skyline.
Say we thick tarred with noise.
Say sun love this skin long,
we ossify dark.
we crack seethe in fault lines.

Say look, we want whole worlds in our mouths
like baby Krishna. Say we feet first plant.
swell to split this battlefield.
Say bands of daughters
follow singing.
Say how do we forgive ourselves
for not being suns.

Say like spit. like lost thread.
like victory spiral swan song.
Say first
Rise.

Calamity Jane
Thomas Stewart

The first tomboy I ever met,

the whiskey singing revolver
so certain

a tapdancing jubilee,
swinging punches in saloon brawls

they tried to put her in a dress
in a house in the countryside

by the brook by the haystacks,
by the cows and the apple trees –

The Wild West would not wait

all her life it had tried to spit her out
but she would always call it home,

always ride the carriage into town,

holster her gun, sing:

Calamity!

Calamity!

Jane!

the first rule of ventriloquism club
Paul Howarth

Close to, of course, it's clear
neither voice is true – for that you must
be both ventriloquist and figure: reach
your arm around yourself, push

your hand in through the stoma
concealed in your back, feel and ease
the levers your fingers will find there,
somewhere in the chest, somewhere

near the heart. A simple system of lever
and pulley innervation. Let
your own voice give you voice, your own
breath be fuel enough.

Locker Room Porn
Samuel Green

"...the masculinity exalted through competitive sport is hegemonic, this means that sporting prowess is a test of masculinity even for boys who detest the locker room. Those who reject the hegemonic patterns have to fight or negotiate their way out." R. W. Connell

The sweat, adhesive between my shirt&chest, damp cotton
weighing on my aching legs. Collapsing down, my feet
get stuck between wooden bench slats,
their frames coated in glossy baby blue (for the boys changing room).
Through the filters of my eyelashes, below a tilted head,
I observe their bravado: the bantering boys
punching others' bruises, loose fitted P.E. shorts are thrown at faces,
fledglings flaunting delusions of pecs and biceps that I see too.
I button up, over sports kit, over my lanky body, Windsor knot
too tight, undid shoe lace. I bolt from the shower-block torrent
as the heat pools at the base of my belly, *The Beast's Reprise*,
the cowardly lion sharpening the notes to his *I Want*,
more than courage on his appetite. I'm stumbling over my shoes,
poorly navigating the breezeblock corridors, scattered
with the dried leaves and football-boot dirt from the outside,
and my body is the dribbled ball knocking over the cones.

Young men line themselves against the boundary wall,
elastic waistbands below ass cheeks, belts hanging at knees;
they belt the ball at each other, slapping their skin
...who can last the longest. (A game of who can last)
They're tackled into the grassy beds, tugging at each other's' shirts,
pinning limbs like location markers of subjugations,
each a colony of their strengths, snapping stick figures/wire men.

I sashay home to my pine-wood residing, where wavering winds
>are the organist
playing the branches as the accompaniment to my lion's lament.
I plant my thighs between roots, bare back against the vast trunk,
and open a new tab on my phone:
>>The jock with veiny hands pushes the head of his faggot
>>down, harsh lighting drawing on the lines of his abs. He
>>punishes him for looking, he kisses him to hurt him, fucks
>>him to pleasure him.
Lichen climbs up my legs, mushrooms sprout beneath my armpits,
>and I bid
to sing my eleven o'clock number to the drawing open of my velvet
>eyelids.

exquisite corpse
Jack Cooper

whose child is this / a boy / nothing like the son needing more than I give / a boy / holding onto grudges like coins / a boy with the anger of a man / of his father / a boy / unspooling from my hips / from sexlessness / a boy / almost a man now / my son asleep on a pile of milk teeth

Common
Natalie Whittaker

New College, Oxford, second year 'halfway dinner'; by now, I'm nearly halfway comfortable with being here, but then Michael D who studies Theology announces at me — and the table in general — *Your voice has a very common twang*. For a few seconds I burn silence, then make light — *It might be common in Bexleyheath, but it's pretty fucking rare round here!* — cauterising the hit with South London flare; no one likes us, we don't care. But I cared. *Common.* Common like there's loads of me, the loose change of me rattling around in pockets; bits of me down the backs of sofas, a smear of me trodden into carpet. So I took offence, then smiled and took drinks in a candlelit common room

and eighteen months later I'm standing with the man who runs a graduate training scheme in advertising, and he's telling me: *You're so surprising, so refreshing; you sound like you should be working in JD Sports or something, then I find out you went to Oxford!* then he frowns and says he's *worried* — had I *taken offence?* and I wonder how much offence one person is allowed to take, and just how common this feeling is.

A poem for Alina that is not called 'Rain'
Tim Kiely

That would be clichéd. I won't write one,
at least not without learning
a new word for it:
                         deszcz.

Learned for the way the halting delivery
is merciful, for the likes of me,
plodding its iterations: *pada deszcz;*
                obfity deszcz
                także ulewny deszcz;

my muddy pronunciation slowing down
the confrontation with the fact
that the language will not translate one-to-one
from a tongue where it seems each gem-soft sphere
is afforded recognition: *deszcz.*

I like it. I relish promises,
as a non-Polish speaker, of
onomatopoeia, downpour, *deszcz.*

The consonants are Biblical,
the ones that Larkin would have used
for his furious, devout *deszcz,*

a mouthing to drown in, a doom of sky,
ardour of pavements and thunderhead
bursting upon the earth as *deszcz*,

or even the gentle reminder, when we are caught
without our umbrellas, crowned in reflections,
only to be. Even though I know now
that the last sound remains unstressed

it persists as a finger to the lips,
                        a *deszcz*, attention tending towards

a joyous silence, broken only
by the sound of falling....

Valencia
Estelle Birdy

Orange blossoms fill my head in the dark and warmth after snow
Yankee Russian Jewish Teacher says it is awesome to see you
and you warrior

She lives in stone on a cobbled street where it is sunny no rain
I watch the waves alone there's a massive undertow and I would
drown but still

I listen and learn here are the fruits of your labour and here
are the chems to make these plants perfect don't use them
and the beautiful

old town sighs with nasties on its fraying edges and the Spaniards
wear scarves but it's hot and pretend everything's different now
in the churches

arms and legs and fingers and heads hang like hams and I salivate
welcome to the horror hall of Christ I think I'll leave it thanks
and eat elsewhere

twenty tapas and a procession of small grimy statues with music
more body parts and demons attacking the near dead
this is tasty

at dawn we carry blankets to the shore and throw shapes and drink
tea and sympathy and watch the orange rise above the purple I need
money she says

Elena plays piano she is beautiful between worlds and she is pulled
to her mother who kisses and loves her and I run three miles
to the sea

The Hepworth
Maria Leonard

The curve of white marble furling
like the pumpkin halves gutted
for you; the spinal cord tensity of that squat
sculpture against the afternoon sun
a reminder of your commanding voice, tight-

lipped and alert as I mumbled at tomatoes,
cut with inept fingers, the muscular
meat off-cuts granted impunity
under your delicacy -

    those fingertips now a fleshy shadow
against Hepworth's designs (a culmination
of modern boredom, the lithographer's
knife and adroitly fingered wire); summoning

a home, ours, which came
mutely under forks crashing against plates
and after pouring borscht down each gullet;
a product of our hands.

Each pumpkin skin had crisped as
you absently reminded me to wash
the tomatoes, all feverish crimson and
warped bleeding,

prompting my lower abdomen to wonder
when those fingertips would turn gesture to touch,
where words like moist forefingers would become
themselves against red folds,
supple and pliant.
Beside the vacant wall the sculpture stood
like an open hand, unflinching.

Big and Clever
Miles Fagge

My fingers are bone and I worked them
That way. A bastardised perfection in the
Midst of this fucking grey. Not big. Not clever.
Never claim to be either just aching limbs
And feeling cheap I am worth so much
More than they pay but cold is cold and
Heat costs. My fingers are bone and my
Eyes are fucking grey. It all seems big and
Not clever at least it casts a big enough
Shadow. We search out words and so often
Fall short so it is all hum and
Misconstrued inaccuracy. I broke my back
And every day it is a new little piece making
It easier to bend over backwards but not so
Easy because the world is heavy and big
And clever and cleverer than me. My fingers
Are bone and dust and my lungs are ash and
It is dark because light is hard to find and
Expensive and my fingers are dust and my
Back is broken and I don't get paid what I
Should they couldn't fucking afford me but
They do.
                       Cut price bastardised perfection.

life is good beneath the leaves
Shaun Hill

the way some people split a tenner with no fear,
life is good beneath the leaves... the wind
shimmies her pom-poms & you can hear it—

each twig a fossil of light on this dizzy
spinning earth... where worms tickle dirt,
& fur coats are worn by fungi, & women bow

into arrows up the blue path through the trees,
on red bikes in the breeze, ticking toward
the sun to sing: *we are one, we are one, I love me.*

Butch
Roma Havers

When your mother tells you   you   'used to be so'
are no longer beautiful she uses the phrase   you used to be so you

used to be so like you

in the wings of Swan Lake, a ballerino's ruffled thigh
teems temporary as a pinata

like a pinata   your body is always in contention with itself

like a waxwork of a washerwoman holding a jug
it is difficult to keep up with you

how your hair sloughs off like the loosening
of cygnet quills   how swans are flightless when moulting
             how a female swan is called a pen

                           a pen feels like
         brothers taking human form fifteen minutes every evening

this is not

like you

        she is not sure you are strong enough to hoist to disjoint

but you like most when your uncle shakes your hand in the abattoir

    when you have poached an unmarked royal swan

    it is difficult
    it is difficult to imagine
    It is difficult to imagine you
    It is difficult to imagine you hacking up something she loves

like you are now a brutalist
rendition of your father the oddity of always
        being somehow him
               diving perfectly but never silent into a pool
              you might rather be that than the portly
girl trying to grapple the wet hair from her mouth so she can breathe

when your mother says you used to be so

beautiful she might be saying 'I am so glad you still want to be a woman,
I couldn't bear to raise someone who didn't want to be a woman'

and I want say – this is what loving womanhood could look like
a perfect butchering of something else.

Plantain
Isabelle Baafi

1

Pick one with black skin. Plucked before it was ripe, left to darken on a windowsill, or in a garage crate, or in the pantry corner where secrets are born.

2

Make sure it's plump. Squeeze it at the curves; weigh its resistance to your touch. Slice it with your tongue. Or, if this is your first time, the fingernail you use to pick your teeth. Keep the peel. Put it under your pillow, and you will never be fruitless.

3

Any oil will do, but make sure it knows its role. Make sure it knows it's not water. Put just enough for each piece to tread the surface. Don't drown them. Give them hope. The hopeful taste the best.

4
In the heat they will hiss, and some will spit.
They will gather at the fringes. Hide their bruising
darkness. Some will be too weak and fall apart.
Others will be hard around the edges. Do not
be suspicious. This is how they endure the fire.

5
Serve on a banana leaf, with the yams you pounded
earlier, the ewe you slaughtered silently from behind.

the bull symbol in 'A'
Jade Cuttle

"A" first reared its ox-head and two horns under the crack of a whip around 1800 BC in ancient Semitic ⅋ ploughing sense to the surface of the mind's muddy fields.

***

It took millennia for ⅋ to muster the courage to run away. Still ⅋ became "A" and my tongue twists wildly in excitement.

***

Ah barely used t' no'ice 't, m' tongue, slumped 'neath a blank't a' spit an' short Yorkshuh vowels. *"D'y wan' owt from t' chippy?"* But then 't eight'een 't was ripped out, m' tongue, pinned t' whiteboard an' measured 'gainst those a' m' class.

***

A*AAAB. Hats off, young lady, welcome to Cambridge, your new abode. *Hinc lucem et pocula sacra.* How frightfully *infra dig* to read *lingua et litteris* anywhere else than the best institution in the world. Please, I pray, do *try* to make yourself feel at home.

***

Assessed on average saliva production, I scored higher than my peers: 1.5 litres a day as words retreated silently down my throat. But lagging behind in length, it was the vowel span I couldn't master.

The vowels I stole were too bulky to speak or swallow.

***

Th/e:/y j/a:/mm/e:/d /o:/p/e:/n my j/a:/w /a:/s /i:/f w/i:/th st/i:/cks /a:/nd l/i:/k/e:/ /a:/ w/i:/nd/o:/w st/u:/ck /o:/n /a·/ r/ʌː/ɛty l/ɑ./tʌ/lɪ f/oː/r yu/aː/ɪs /lː/ c/o://u:/ldn't cl/o:/s/e:/.

***

Neighbours being neighbours, they pointed and passed comment, so I prised the sticks out // and papered over the cuts. The inside of my cheeks are r/a:/w.

***

Together, m' tongue an' I, w' strained friggin' 'ard, epiglottis t't tip, buildin' a /pa:/ / t'wards a better version o' m' self; stretching my [a] into an /a:/ we pr/a:/cticed the eleg/a:/nt pirouettes of the prim/a:/ ballerin/a:, performing the C/a:/mbridge version of "Oxford English" to /a:/crowd that couldn't c/a:/re less.

***

But where are you *really* from?

***

We pulled so many muscles trying to prove this skin a shawl, a layer of mud I could lose in the wash, beneath which a well-educated white girl would be keeping warm: a Kinder Surprise translated into human form ◌. .

It's not my tongue that lacks temper: intelligent domesticated beast, like the runway ox & 'ts sick t' back teeth a' pullin' carts whose cargo in't 'ts own.

***

'ts even sick a' pullin' cargo 't is 'ts own.

***

This tongue has lived the barrier of language too long. I can no longer call this mouth my own.

***

[A]h cl[a]mbuh over't Yorkshuh vowels [a]h used t'master, dr[a]m[a]tisin' m' desp'r[a]te se[a]rch for s[a]fe [a]n' st[a]ble ground. But sn[a]ggin' 'pon their sh[a]rp wire edges, 'ts [a] complete sh[a]mbles, [a]h c[a]n't gerrin.

***

Mistaken for enemy forces, I've fenced myself out from my mouth and into a minefield. We seek refuge in both rough and more rounded sounds, but whichever one we choose is an insult against the truth. Each word threatens to blow the cover on who I really am.

***

And so my tongue keeps its distance, knowing that language, left to rot like a slumped wood stack, will splinter at the touch.

***

What else is there to do but pick up a pen, pitch my black tent upon the white page and crawl inside? I've locked myself out my own mouth. Deeds and documents prove nothing.

***

I peg down the punctuation then gather flint to light a fire. I pray this fire will keep me warm, but my language will no longer light. It refuses to welcome these unlawful, thieving hands.

Journal Fragments '82
Dale Booton

met a young guy down by Piccadilly station   told him
he was beautiful   he was

mom called again today   couldn't put her off for a
fifth time   said she's coming down because she wants to meet
David   too late   it's been over for a week

there's a new cocktail at Dickie's   the drunken queen   delicious

had my 30th tonight   everyone was there   music   beer   cheers and
David   he'd forgotten   of course   just came to
collect the last of his things

Pete has found a great place in Soho   said it's to die for

Marty came by   Will's sick   really sick   he can't stand without
fainting   has no idea what's causing it but it's bad

fuck   got called daddy last night   I'm officially dead   RIP me

Will's getting worse   mad fever and weird purple
spots all over his body   no not spots   lesion things that grow

David came around   bled his heart out   we fucked
and he said he'd call me in the week   we'll see if he does

it's AIDS   they don't really know what it is
but it's a mean motherfucker   Will's got it which means
Marty has it too

they're trying to cure it   so they say   like they actually care

Will's dead   Marty found him this morning

David came around   I've never seen him so pale   he has it
too   told me to get checked but I feel fine   I'm not
going to worry 'cause worrying makes it worse

mom's been calling all day   read about the gay cancer and
now she's scared   she said she knew something bad would happen

Will's funeral today   Marty stayed last night   got shitfaced to cope

met a cute guy down by the gents   he was huge   nice ass too

Marty's dead   hung himself   I can't stop crying

everyone came to pay their respects   said he was
too young to go

I don't want to leave the flat   how long have we got

sat in the clinic for an hour
just sat
I couldn't stand up and ask to be tested   felt dirty   scared

David came over   his new lover Sam has it   he's twenty-one   oh god

sat in the clinic again   it was too much   I don't want to know if   no

mom called   Jen's having a New Year's party and
wants to know if I'll be able to make it

phones been ringing all day   more deaths   more diagnoses

sat in the clinic again with Pete   he held my hand   told me it will all
    be fine

I've got it

David called   mom called   David called again   I ignored them
both   I don't want to talk to them   I don't want to
talk to anyone

they have new information but still no cure

Pete's been diagnosed David's dead Sam's dying Rich is going
    crazy Thom
has no idea where he is Phil is coughing up his blood Brian's funeral
is tomorrow Ted's the day after and mine is to come

this has to stop

The Gift Shop Elegies #9: Elegy with Exhibition Booklet for 'Coming Out: Sexuality, Gender & Identity' (Walker Art Gallery, Liverpool; Birmingham Museum and Art Gallery)
Zosia Kuczynska

In mid-December, 2016, Dad was back in hospital, having come home for what we'd all assumed would be for good but which ended up as something like four days. There's little I remember of that time apart from being alone inside a house I'd decorated wall to wall with home-made decorations as a way to mark his coming back to us—a seasonal aesthetic which will now forever be associated with the shock and hopelessness of turned events, like being mugged and left for dead on the set of a pantomime.

>I have learned what needs needling together
>and what does not;
>what constitutes a wound
>and what does not—

Around that time, I'm sick of my own mouth, the scarred skin all around it, and my lack of energy to use it—whether in speech or in expressive grimacing; resent the seasonal and gendered expectations that it should find something to smile about. I take a red lipstick and paint my mouth as red and wide as the missing part of a post-box; take photographs in which I neither smile nor cry behind a drawn-on scarlet sash. The natural lip, of course, is visible, because this clownish lip is far too broad either to hide the contours of my face or to animate with acrobat emotions; still, it has allowed me to perform my sense of the simultaneous absence and redundant presence of my stilled mouth, and I think the photographs are beautiful.

> I'd begun to tell you this
> when you died of wounds,
> needled back together
> and to sleep.

When, some months later, having been bereaved, I then attempt a Bette Davis lip, it doesn't work because my cupid's bow is prominent enough to catch the light. I compensate by taking photographs in 'noir', which gives a greater contrast to the lipstick; I get curious; I draw a full moustache that fills my upper lip and try to find my dad. It occurs to me how much it must have hurt his feelings when—having accidentally shaved off his moustache—his teenage daughters wept to see his face because they'd never seen it in their lives. He grew it back as soon as possible.

> A haunted face
> need not be an unhappy one:
> there is playfulness,
> sometimes; questions asked
> that must be asked
> before they can be answered.

Almost all that I would like to say on death and drag has already been said far more succinctly by drag queen Sasha Velour. In a short essay, 'What I've learned about death as a drag queen', Velour acknowledges the inherent potential for elegy in a queer art form whose practitioners, accustomed to accommodating ghosts, will often draw on a parent's example or wardrobe in their first foray into performing gender. The essay now accompanies a comic in which Velour looks through her mother's closet and asks 'are these things mine?' before selecting a turquoise suit her mother used to wear and wearing it to scatter her mother's ashes.

> This was not your pain, nor this
> your pain relief: your ostracism was
> the everyday ostracism of dying; morphine
> would only have taken your breath away.

'[D]rag is', Mark Doty writes, 'a city/ to cover our nakedness'. 'Look how I rhyme', he writes, 'with the skyscraper's/ padded sawtooth shoulders', the way a sonneteer will set themselves to rhyme with the unattainable in which they clothe their lyric selves—as if to say, like Doty, 'I want/ not his product but his display'. The lyric I is also a form of drag: take Sylvia Plath, all 'cow-heavy and floral' in the wake of childbirth—her nightgown loud with performativity and Victoriana as she stumbles through the effacement of motherhood in her poem 'Morning Song'. Take inadvertent drag king Michael Longley, who puts on all the armours of ancient Greece and Flanders combined so he can talk about his father. Take the elegist, who, not unlike the sonneteer, becomes an 'I' that queers the pronoun of the speaking self and says 'I am not I; pity the tale of me'.

> There is a collective history
> I am in the process of inheriting,
> gingerly: would I dissect this painting;
> would I repurpose your shirts?

Sasha Velour excels at elegiac lip-syncs that function as a commentary on drag, and is known for performing bald in tribute to her mother. In one significant example of this, Velour performs

'This Woman's Work' as recorded by Kate Bush. Initially, she drapes herself in white; she then projects herself onto herself, her various looks, before settling on her mother's turquoise suit, a fuchsia bra half-showing underneath, and a pair of fuchsia gloves with an ostrich trim. Sasha tears away the covering, revealing herself to be wearing the self-same outfit; her projected self comes out and steps aside and turns her back as Sasha turns her head to sing to her. 'Give me these moments back', she mouths through glittered lips, 'give me your hand'.

> 'Can love remember the question and the answer?'
> If the question is whether things can wither
> and attain their own peculiar significance,
> like flowers that have dried behind a door
> through which they have long been visible
> to anyone with eyes, then yes—the answer is yes.

When I sit Dad down on the sofa, less than a month before he goes to have the operation that will ultimately dwindle him to ash and tell him that it's Bi Visibility Day, I haven't learned the difference between bisexuality and pansexuality, which is my term of choice— an undramatic redefining, but it fits the bill. And coming out to Dad is anticlimactic, despite the fact that he's the last to know, but here's the thing: the way he slaps the sofa cushions in indignation swells my heart with its idiosyncrasy; when I make myself visible to him, so to speak, he only splutters, 'Nobody ever tells me anything!'

WORKS CITED:
Bush, Kate, 'This Woman's Work', *The Sensual World* (EMI, 1989).
Doty, Mark, 'Crêpe de Chine', in *Atlantis* (London: Jonathan Cape, 1996), pp. 65–67.
Longley, Michael, *Collected Poems* (London: Jonathan Cape, 2007).
Plath, Sylvia, 'Morning Song', in *Collected Poems*, ed. by Ted Hughes (London: Faber and Faber, 1989), pp. 156–157.

Sidney, Philip, 'Sonnet 45', *Astrophil and Stella*, in *Sir Philip Sidney: The Major Works*, ed. and intr. by Katherine Duncan-Jones (Oxford: Oxford University Press, 2002), p. 170.

Velour, Sasha, '"WHAT NOW?" COMIC', first published in InkBRICK #4 (2015) <http://sasha-steinberg-f2n3.squarespace.com/whatnow> [accessed 19 April 2019]

---, 'Sasha Velour | "This Woman's Work" | NIGHTGOWNS', 20 January 2017 <https://www.youtube.com/watch?v=111m9mp5eiVs> [accessed 19 April 2019]

ARTWORKS

Annie Wright (born 1952)
Hiding the Wound: Homage to Mr Freud
Made in 1979
Gelatin silver print
20 x 13.7 cm
Arts Council Collection, South Bank Centre, London

David Hurn (born 1934)
A Gay Threesome Pose before going to a Local Gay Ball
Taken in 1970
Gelatin silver print
38 x 25 cm
Arts Council Collection, Southbank Centre, London

Derek Jarman (1942–1994)
Morphine
Painted in 1992
Oil paint on photocopies on canvas
215.5 x 179 cm
Arts Council Collection, South Bank Centre, London

Anya Gallaccio (born 1963)
can love remember the question and the answer?
Made in 2003
Mahogany, glass and flowers
275 x 143 cm
Arts Council Collection, South Bank Centre, London

Dust
Jemima Hughes

You were created in this universe and you want to fit in?
Brewed in the heart of an explosion. Stardust.

A potential five hundred million planets
capable of supporting life, and we can't all support each other on one.
A single quality (and I do mean quality) receives hate,
when 99.9% of species are already gone.

You are a black body.
A star,
absorbing all radiant energy,
emitting much more by far.

They believe they are the Sun,
which is to say, you are bigger and brighter.
The human eye factors in surrounding colours, so the appearance
    is whiter,
but the Sun is a green star.

A jealous ball of raging fire.

Your light breaks through turbulent atmosphere
illuminating the way for others,
the twinkle in your eye reveals every deflection,
causing a change of intensity in your colours.

...

They move like the billions of lifeforms on their skin
feast on champagne and caviar,
swim in oceans accommodating two hundred thousand different
    viruses,
but won't gaze upon the beauty that you are.

Scared,
Scared they're going to catch on,
catch themselves viewing rainbows in black and white.
Supernovas brought elements essential for survival,
and you are essential for this world to get survival right.

If someone looks at you like they want to fix you,
they will fall through the cracks,
not all star systems are binary,
and the cosmos exists naturally, it does not have to apologise for
    the way it acts.

Are you a galaxy?
With a black hole at the centre of you?
Black holes are very, very cold,
but galaxies will not be consumed.

Gravitational attraction pulls in matter,
this force works to ground you,
try to keep a stable orbit
until this force of nature is through.

One hundred and forty billion (or so) galaxies,
you're not alone in this gloom.
And you're about to be on fire
because when a flame is at its hottest, it appears blue.

13.8 billion years old
and getting more interesting by the day,
your age adds to your wonder,
it doesn't take your worth away.

A teaspoon of neutron star weighs
about ten million tonnes,
and your weight, or size,
doesn't dictate your levels of attraction.

More than twenty-four time zones means
you and your anxiety made it on time,
when you look into the starry sky you're looking deep into the past,
so your punctuality after sunset is sublime.

Outer space is open to interpretation
and your silence is of tremendous value,
needing spectacles doesn't make you a spectacle
when 95% of the universe is still out of view.

Survival on Earth is unnecessarily difficult,
and lives are so good at ruining lives,
but if we judge those who judge us we resolve nothing,
accepting our self is how we survive.

You see, you stand out against the back drop of this universe,
and almost all ordinary matter is empty space,
if someone struck a match on the moon, astronomers could spot
    the flame,
the right people will see you and your qualities will be embraced.

    ...

Finding flaws in someone else doesn't make our own less visible,
throwing shade won't change the shade of someone's skin,
if you touch two pieces of the same type of metal together
in the vacuum of space, they will fuse.

And rainbows have always created a happiness within.

The static of a retro television
displays the Big Bang afterglow,
we won't always have the correct channel of thought,
but the reason is bigger than we know.

The Sun rages, but it can still bring warmth and light,
and space has enough space for us all to progress.
At the bare bones of it we are all the same,
and if we are all simply dust, shouldn't we clean up our mess?

www.vervepoetrypress.com
@VervePoetryPres
mail@vervepoetrypress.com

THE POETS

Isabelle Baafi is a writer and poet. Her work has been published in *The Caribbean Writer, Allegro, Moko Magazine, Kalahari Review* and elsewhere. She was recently admitted to the London Library's Emerging Writers Programme, and performed at the Battersea Arts Centre's Homegrown Festival. She is currently working on her debut poetry collection

Estelle Birdy is a writer, yoga teacher and mother of four, living and working in Dublin. She recently graduated from the Creative Writing Masters programme in UCD. Her work has been shortlisted in several competitions and has been published in *The Squawkback, Sonder Midwest* and *Heartland Anthology* to name a few. Her work, both poetry and prose, often focuses on the absurd and dark in our everyday experience.

Dale Booton is a twenty-four year old English teacher from Birmingham. He has a degree in Psychology with Criminology from Birmingham City University. When he isn't teaching, he is either writing, researching queer history, or reading comics. At school, he encourages students to write their own poetry, working with Young Writers to give his students a platform to show off their growing talent.

Jhilmil Breckenridge is a poet, writer and activist. She is the Founder of Bhor Foundation, an Indian charity, which is active in mental health advocacy, the trauma informed approach, and enabling other choices to heal apart from the biomedical model. She advocates Poetry as Therapy and is working on a few initiatives, both in the UK and India, taking this into prisons and asylums. She is working on a PhD in Creative Writing in the UK. Her debut poetry collection *Reclamation Song* was initially released in India in late May 2018, through Red River Press.

Claire Collison won the inaugural Women Poets' Prize, 2018. She came second in Resurgence and Hippocrates prizes, and has been shortlisted for Flambard, Poetry Business, Rialto Pamphlet, Primers5, and Bridport prizes. Recent poems appear in *Second Place Rosette: Poems about Britain* (Emma Press), *The Valley Press Anthology of Prose Poetry, Butcher's Dog, Finished Creatures,* and *The Rialto*. Claire was awarded ACE funding for Truth is Beauty, her single-breasted life modelling monologue, and her participatory Intimate Tours of Breasts. She is actively involved in Poets4ThePlanet. clairecollison.com

A member of Highgate Poets, **Jack Cooper** has been longlisted in the National Poetry Competition, and published by The Oxford Magazine, ASH, and Young Poets Network. He is currently undertaking a PhD in embryonic cell migration at the University of Warwick. He can be found on Twitter at @JackCooper666

Natalie Crick (Newcastle) has poems published in *The Moth, Banshee, Bare Fiction, New Welsh Review* and elsewhere. She has an MA in Writing Poetry and is studying for an MPhil in Creative Writing at Newcastle University. Natalie has read her poetry at Newcastle Poetry Festival 2018/19. Twice nominated for the Pushcart Prize, her poetry has been shortlisted for The Anthony Cronin International Poetry Award 2018, commended in the Hippocrates Open Awards for Poetry and Medicine 2019 and runner-up in the PBS & Mslexia Women's Poetry Competition 2018. Natalie's collaborative pamphlet is *Co-Incidental 5* (Black Light Engine Room Press, 2019).

Jade Cuttle holds a first-class honours degree in Modern & Medieval Languages & Literature from the University of Cambridge and an MA in Creative Writing (Poetry) from the University of East Anglia. She has been commissioned to write poetry for BBC Radio 3's 'Words and Music', BBC's Contains Strong Language performance festival, and for the BBC Proms' Official Guide. Jade is an editor at Ambit and judged the Costa Book Awards 2019 (Poetry). Selected as a Ledbury Poetry Festival Emerging Poetry Critic and winning Best Reviewer (Editor's Choice) in the Saboteur Awards 2018, Jade reviews widely. Her criticism regularly appears in publications such as the Guardian, Times Literary Supplement and The Telegrap. Fusing metaphor with melody, Jade released her debut eco-themed album of poem-songs 'Algal Bloom' with funding and support from the PRS foundation and Make Noise in January 2020. She currently works full-time at The Poetry Society and is a tutor at Poetry School.

Miles Fagge grew up in the West Midlands before studying English Literature at the University of Sussex. Whilst living in Brighton he began to write regularly and perform at events in the city. Since graduating he has moved back to the West Midlands to work in left-wing politics, continuing to campaign against austerity and the politics of division, whilst maintaining his passion for poetry.

Samuel Green is a Creative Writing graduate of Brunel University London. He was raised in the valleys of South Wales and now lives in London working in TV Broadcasting. His poems have appeared in multiple anthologies from the Hillingdon Literary Festival and regularly touch upon themes of masculinity.

Roma Havers, 24, is a Manchester-based queer writer, performer and facilitator. Her favourite critic called her work "LSD for nerds from the genderf***ed child of Elizabeth Bishop and Doctor Seuss" and her worst said it was "a bit thinky for me." She has been commissioned by Young Identity, HOMEmcr, Manchester Histories and MIF, and has performed for radio, television, nationally and internationally. In July 2019 she was poet in residence for MMU Special Collections Library. Her first solo show 'Bolted' debuted with UKYA in February 2019, and her second 'LOB' will launch with GMLGBT Consortium in January 2020.

Shaun Hill has read his work across the country in beds, bars, and festivals like WOMAD, Shambala, and UK Young Artist's Takeover 2019. He is a Young Poet with the Birmingham Hippodrome and a mentee with Nine Arches Press. You can find his poetry in *Magma*, *Under The Radar*, and on BBC Radio 4. Find him online at warmbloodedthing.co.uk.

Paul Howarth is originally from Cheshire and now lives in Suffolk with his wife and two sons. In between raising a family and his work leading on content for Suffolk Libraries, a charity that promotes social inclusion and wellbeing through reading and other cultural experiences, he tries to fit in some writing. Paul's poems have featured in various magazines and anthologies, most recently in *Anthology 84* (Verve Poetry Press) and *The Result is What You See Today: Poems About Running* (Smith|Doorstop).

Jemima Hughes is a multi-slam winning performance poet from Birmingham engaged in an ongoing mental health battle. She turned to writing poetry to express herself at a time when her verbal communication was minimal, consequently finding a new passion. These days, Jemima has found her voice again, mastered timing and rhythm, and has travelled across the UK and Ireland to headline multiple spoken word events. Her debut collection, *Unorthodox*, is forthcoming from Verve Poetry Press.

Christopher M James, a dual British/French national, grew up in West London and has lived and worked for forty five years in Human Resources, in France, Italy and Thailand. He started writing three years ago after retirement and has since been a prize winner in several competitions (Sentinel, Yeovil, Stroud, Poets meet Politics, Hanna Greally...), notably winning the Maria Edgeworth Literary award and the Bailieborough Poetry Prize in 2019, and the Earlyworks Poetry Prize in 2018. He has also been published in a variety of anthologies (Live Canon, WoLF, Canterbury Poet of the Year ...)

'Tim Kiely is a criminal barrister and poet based in London. His work has been published in: Lunar Poetry; *South Bank Poetry; 'The Morning Star' Spontaneous Poetics; Ink, Sweat & Tears* and *Under the Radar*. He has featured in the Emma Press anthology, *Everything That Can Happen* and his poem *It Is the Trees* was a Highly Commended entry in the 2019 Gingko Prize Anthology for Ecopoetry. He is a member of the Poets Versus collective, Chair of the Tower Hamlets Green Party and will be running as the London Assembly Candidate for City and East in 2020.

Karl Knights is a freelance journalist, essayist and poet. His work has appeared in *The Guardian, The Dark Horse* and *The North*. He is twenty-three and lives in Suffolk.

Zosia Kuczyńska is the author of *Pisanki* (The Emma Press, 2017). Her work has been published in *The White Review, The Tangerine,* and *Poetry Ireland Review*. In 2019, she was shortlisted for the Mairtín Crawford Award for Poetry and highly commended in the Patrick Kavanagh Poetry Award. She is currently an IRC postdoctoral research fellow at University College Dublin.

Prerana Kumar is an Indian spoken word artist doing her MA in English at Durham University. She is the winner of the Say Owt Slam 2018 and won the Verve Poet of the Slam prize for best individual performance at UniSlam 2019. She was a BBC WordsFirst Finalist (2019), as well as a finalist for the Asia House Poetry Slam 2019. She has performed at spoken-word events across the UK. She has been published in *The Writer's Cafe, The Verve Community Anthology,* and *Use Words First*. Her poetry revolves around identity, love, loss and occasionally, a healthy dose of nyctophilia.

Maria Leonard is a writer and producer working across the arts, digital culture and tech.

Stephanie Papa lives in Paris, France. She is a Phd student and professor at Université Paris 13-Sorbonne Cité. She was poetry editor of *Paris Lit Up* magazine for 3 years. Her work has been published in *The Stinging Fly, World Literature Today, Magma Poetry, It All Radiates Outwards* anthology (Verve Poetry Press), *Nicho, NOON*, among others. She organizes writing workshops and readings in Paris for international poets.

Jack Parlett recently completed a PhD on poetry and cruising and is currently a Junior Research Fellow in English at University College, Oxford, where he is writing a book about the queer literary history of Fire Island. His debut poetry pamphlet, *same blue, different you*, will publish with Broken Sleep Books in August 2020. His poetry has appeared in *Hotel, Blackbox Manifold* (with Anne Stillman as 'Otto & Gisel'), *Visual Verse* and the *BFI Flare zine*, and he has written reviews and essays for *Literary Hub, Poetry London, the Cambridge Humanities Review* and *Dazed and Confused*.

Eleanor Penny is a writer, journalist, poet and teacher. She's a three-times Barbican Young Poet, twice shortlisted for Young People's Poet Laureate for London. Commissions include the Barbican, the Poetry School, the Cinema Museum. She's an editor at Novara Media, and the host of poetry podcast 'Bedtime Stories for the End of the World' and 'Politics Matters' on FUBAR Radio. Her work has appeared in numerous outlets including New Statesman, Verso Books and the Independent. Her first book is forthcoming with flipped eye.

Michael Saunderson lives and works in Warwick, managing an international team of IT people. His poems have appeared on paper in *Under the Radar*, online at *Here Comes Everyone* and out loud as a featured poet for @PGRpoetry spoken word events.

Thomas Stewart is a welsh writer based in Edinburgh. His debut poetry pamphlet *empire of dirt* is published by Red Squirrel Press and was part of the Poetry Book Society's summer selections. His work has been published at *Oh Comely, The Glasgow Review of Books, Ink, Sweat & Tears, Litro Magazine*, among others. He was a writer in residence at Arteles in Finland. He can be found on Twitter @ThomasStewart08.

Kat Payne Ware is a poet from Bristol. She graduated cum laude in Literature and Creative Writing from the University of Birmingham in 2019, and is currently reading for an MA in Creative Writing Poetry at the University of East Anglia. Her poetry has been published in *Brixton Review of Books*.

Hilary Watson is a graduate of the University of Warwick Writing Programme and was a Jerwood/Arvon Mentee. Her poems have recently appeared in *The Interpreter's House, Butcher's Dog, Impossible Archetype* and *The Emma Press Anthology of Contemporary Gothic Verse*. She was shortlisted for the Troubadour International Poetry Prize 2018 and the inaugural I'll Show You Mine Prize 2019. She lives in Cardiff with her girlfriend.

Natalie Whittaker is a secondary school teacher and poet who lives in South East London. Her debut pamphlet *Shadow Dogs* was published by ignitionpress in 2018. She has recently had work published in *Poetry News* and *The Valley Press Anthology of Prose Poetry*.

ALSO AVAILABLE FROM VERVE POETRY PRESS

Eighty Four:
Poems on Male Suicide, Vulnerability, Grief and Hope

Edited and with an introduction by
Helen Calcutt

Eighty Four is an anthology of poetry on the subject of male suicide in aid of CALM (campaign against living miserably). Poems have been donated to the collection by Andrew McMillan, Salena Godden, Anthony Anaxagorou, Katrina Naomi, Ian Patterson, Carrie Etter Peter Raynard and Joelle Taylor while a submissions window yielded many excellent poems on the subject from both known and hitherto unknown poets we are thrilled to have been made aware of.

Curated by poet Helen Calcutt, Eighty-Four showcases human vulnerability in all its forms. From the baby in the bath who knows daddy is gone, to the woman whose father haunts her through the window, here is a diverse collection of voices, delicately speaking the intense difficulties of the human predicament, courageously engaging with the profound impact that male suicide is having on all of us. There's a glittering strength to this volume, because of the honesty from which its poems have been created, giving this book the truth it was seeking.

This books isn't easy but it is powerful and true. Well worth a read and a thought.

ISBN: 978 1 912565 13 9
108 pages • 216 x 138 • 42 poems
£9.99

ABOUT VERVE POETRY PRESS

Verve Poetry Press, now in its second year, is focussing intently on meeting a local need in Birmingham - a need for the vibrant poetry scene here in Brum to find a way to present itself to the poetry world via publication. Co-founded by Stuart Bartholomew and Amerah Saleh, it is publishing poets from all corners of the city - poets that represent the city's varied and energetic qualities and will communicate its many poetic stories.

We are also publishing more widely, providing a home for works that, for no fault of their own, are struggling to reach a readership. Our colourful pamphlet series, our spoken word show collections and debut collections that are packing a punch are available to order in all good bookshops and from our own site.

We are a prize-winning press, being named Most Innovative Indie Press at Saboteurs 2019 and winning the coveted Michael Marks Publishers' Awards for pamphlet publishing in the same year.

Like our sister festival, we strive to think about poetry in inclusive ways and embrace the multiplicity of approaches towards this glorious art. So watch this space. Verve Poetry Press means business.

vervepoetrypress.com